PRAISE FOR

Ninety-five Nights of Listening

"*Ninety-five Nights of Listening* is nothing less than a breathtaking debut. Malinda Markham's poems bring with them an exquisite poise and restrained — yet sensual — elegance that is truly remarkable. These are poems filled with respect for the silences of our world. Marked by their discretion, eloquence, and enviable precision, Malinda Markham's poems accrue quietly in their imaginative powers, rising finally to a place of compelling and resonant wisdom." — DAVID ST. JOHN

"Malinda Markham knows a world of wild proliferations. Beginning with sunlight, she finds a thousand suns. Beginning with a cricket's song, she attends the music of the spheres. Here, the senses make sense of all. *Ninety-five Nights of Listening* is a vivid debut, a truly vivifying book." — DONALD REVELL

"As person and poet Malinda Markham seems to have steeped herself in words, native and adopted. She asks, as challenge to the book as well as to the reader, 'Will you remember / This tone, when the actual language is lost?' Malinda Markham's new book is so generously about paying attention that we readers can share, merely by listening, the excitement of a newly reinvented art form — as if poetry is now once again, in her hands, ears, and voice, uniquely itself and like nothing else. That these are beautiful poems is only the beginning of the issue: it is as if they are an invention of a new kind of beauty in and of language." — BIN RAMKE, editor, *Denver Quarterly*

Ninety-five Nights
of Listening

Malinda Markham

A MARINER ORIGINAL
Houghton Mifflin Company
Boston • New York
2002

For information about permission to reproduce selections from
this book, write to Permissions, Houghton Mifflin Company,
215 Park Avenue South, New York, New York 10003.

Visit our Web site: www.houghtonmifflinbooks.com.

Library of Congress Cataloging-in-Publication Data is available.

ISBN 0-618-18928-9

Printed in the United States of America

Book design by Robert Overholtzer

DOC 10 9 8 7 6 5 4 3 2 1

Sincere thanks are due to the editors of the publications in which the following poems first appeared: "Being Glass" and "Because the Cup Is Furred, I Cannot Drink" in *American Letters & Commentary;* "To Recant What Is Needed" in *Colorado Review;* "Oblivion Fruit" in *Comet;* "The Field of Choice. And Choosing." (originally published as "Statuary") in *Conjunctions;* "Woman Bathing" and "Prime Movement and Other Divinations" in *Epoch;* "Postcard—Without Grace" in *The Journal;* "Yield to This" and "Persimmons and a Kind of Regret" (originally published as "Who Does Not Love the Figure Before Them") in *Notre Dame Review;* "Museum Rehearsal" (originally published as "Documentary: Rehearsal") in *Ohio Review;* "Things That Seldom Remain in Place" and "Gift" in *Paris Review;* "Equation" and "Before the River Freezes in Place" in *Phoebe;* "First Received" and "The Perceptible World" in *Poetry Review;* "Conversation in Likeness" in *Quarterly West;* "Affair Ending in Touch" and "The Border Between" in *Rhizome;* "Survival & Disembodied Existence," "Hôtel des Pyrénées," and "Instruction (Against Limited Disaster)" in *Third Coast;* "Being Glass, the Glint of Sun," and "Postcard—a memory carried in the body" in *Faces in the Crowd* (an anthology of Tokyo writers); "Anatomy of Resemblance" and "What Magnitudes Sing Us" in *Verse;* and "Five Stories of Demand" in *VOLT.*

For Gordon Markham

CONTENTS

Bread Loaf and the Bakeless Prizes

Since 1926 the Bread Loaf Writers' Conference has convened every August in the shadow of Bread Loaf Mountain, in Vermont's Green Mountains, where Middlebury College maintains a summer campus. The conference, founded by Robert Frost and Willa Cather — a generation before creative writing became a popular course of study — brings together established poets and prose writers, editors, and literary agents to work with writers at various stages of their careers. Frost's plan for the conference included a faculty of distinguished writers who would "turn from correcting grammar in red ink to matching experience in black ink, experience of life and experience of art." Bread Loaf has stayed true to Frost's original vision, and its vibrancy and energy have helped make it the most respected of the many summer writers' conferences in the nation.

While part of Bread Loaf's reputation was built on the writers associated with it — W. H. Auden, Sinclair Lewis, Wallace Stegner, Katherine Anne Porter, William Carlos Williams, Ralph Ellison, Nelson Algren, Toni Morrison, Adrienne Rich, May Sarton, Archibald MacLeish, Frank O'Connor, and Richard Wright, among others — it has an equally high reputation for finding and supporting writers of promise at the earliest stages of their careers. Eudora Welty, Carson McCullers, Anne Sexton, May Swenson, Russell Banks, Joan Didion, Miller Williams, Richard Yates, Richard Ford, Julia Alvarez, Carolyn Forché, Linda Pastan, Dave Smith, Tess Gallagher, Ellen Bryant Voigt, Andrea Barrett, and Tim O'Brien are some of the poets, novelists, and short story writers who benefited from the scholarships and fellowships Bread Loaf awards annually.

The importance of Bread Loaf for American writers is typified by Julia Alvarez's recollection of her first conference: "I went to Bread Loaf for the first time in 1969 and fell in love with the community of writers . . . All these people talking about nothing but writing, forcing me to think about writing! I aspired to this great society." My own relationship with Bread Loaf began in 1981 when I attended as a scholar, and was renewed in 1986 when I returned as a fellow. These initial opportunities allowed me to work with William Stafford and

Philip Levine, whose influence helped to shape the way I think of myself as a writer. Later, as an associate faculty member, and since 1995 as director, I have repeatedly witnessed the profound effect the eleven days in August have on those who attend. John Ciardi, a former director of the conference and one of its most eloquent spokespeople, liked to say about the Bread Loaf experience that "no great writer ever became one in isolation. Somewhere and sometime, if only at the beginning, he had to experience the excitement and intellectual ferment of a group something like this."

There are many obstacles to a successful literary career, but none is more difficult to overcome than the publication of a first book. The Katharine Bakeless Nason Literary Publication Prizes were established in 1995 to expand Bread Loaf's commitment to the support of emerging writers. Endowed by the LZ Francis Foundation, whose directors wished to commemorate Middlebury College patron Katharine Bakeless Nason and to encourage emerging writers, the Bakeless Prizes launch the publication career of a poet, fiction writer, and creative nonfiction writer annually. Winning manuscripts are chosen in an open, national competition by a distinguished judge in each genre. The winning books are published in August to coincide with the Bread Loaf Writers' Conference, and the authors are invited to participate as Bakeless Fellows.

Since they first appeared in 1996, the winning Bakeless books have been critical successes. As a result, the Bakeless Prizes are coveted among new writers. The fact that Houghton Mifflin publishes these books is significant, for it joins together one of America's oldest and most distinguished literary presses with an equally distinguished writers' conference. The collaboration speaks to the commitment of both institutions to cultivate emerging literary artists in order to ensure a richer future for American writing.

MICHAEL COLLIER
Director, Bread Loaf Writers' Conference

Foreword

In *Ninety-five Nights of Listening*, Malinda Markham notes that "A snake wrapped around a bell / takes the echo with her when she leaves." There is hardly a more apt conceit, a more reverberant and mysterious symbol of Markham's title than this echoing snake.

Scheherezade may be one inspiration for these poems, as the poet tells "stories" over and over to a listening consciousness—but the snake, moving within and out of sound, mysteriously both embodying and escaping the bell's "word," is an even stronger representation of the desire and delight of these poems.

In her poem "Gift," she reinforces this dramatic tactic:

> The birds that chattered in the trees above the school
> have left us with the sound of wings and the smell of smoke
> in our hair. For three nights now, only one star
> has graced the curve of the moon. The sky is silenced.

I am in awe of the unwinding, unwavering magic of these poems. There is a beautiful doubleness of desire here—the desire to make the world known in "storytelling" at the same time as the desire to mask, to shadow, to recloak the world in its natural mystery.

In her poem "Before the River Freezes in Place," this doubleness divides the image in two in this unforgettable, startling vision of a bird struck by lightning:

> Sing me the story where lightning
> divides the tanager in two.
> Each half beak opens, and wind pulls night
> from inside two mouths.
> Are you looking for comfort? No matter
> how you ask it, those two sides of the sky
> do not become one. There are people
> wanting to be covered by night.
> There is a bird-shaped space
> the color of light.

This startling vision, like the image of the reverberant snake, allows poetry to pass through the animate world, allows the reader to witness this thrilling "dividing" passage. The "bird-shaped space / the color of light" is our expectation, our desire for fiction, our hunger for the shape of narrative longing to be filled. Malinda Markham has acknowledged, parodied, and fulfilled this longing in *Ninety-five Nights of Listening*. As judge of the Bakeless poetry prize, I found her book filled with poetic wisdom, tonic insight, and haunting music for the eye and ear—an enchantment and an admonition to all who need "stories" to live.

CAROL MUSKE-DUKES

I

Woman Bathing

1.
Night birds build the yard with their sound:
The porch and lamp and strong columns
of pine. They have filled everything in
but the moon. They are trying.
Soon, all will be level and dark.

2.
To cure poisoned snails in the garden,
grind geraniums into a paste. Feed only
in increments. Do not give enough water
to drown them. Given a chance,
like anything, they will. What child
hasn't practiced dying under water,
listening to waves against the bathtub's
smooth sides? Heart rising,
patient and caged.

3.
Bright parrot, your legs are flutes.
Someone welded a ring about your foot.
Did you try to escape? Three feathers
clipped, you respond
in abbreviated flight. Sing again,
ash-colored beak, and learn to speak
your name. Understand how much
we all love your small face.

4.
Tea is bitter and thick. Crickets in cages
sell for less than a dime.
Where did it come from, this need
to speak like birds in a field,
refining the trees and the fence?

The one who sings the moon shut
finally can sleep. I am waiting.

5.
Straw babies make girls turn away.
So give the dolls faces and names.
I fold paper into boats—perhaps the water
will hold us this time. Press
your hands over your ears. Fish call us down
with silvery tongues. Who else
has stood in this place with no branch
in sight? O cover your ears.
Time runs down the legs as we move.

Instruction (Against Limited Disaster)

I don't know whether they live or die,
These wings like skin
That push time through themselves,
A gift. Long ago, history

Became a list of what pierced us,
Each event with no recollection
Of the last. If a heart could be pressed
Toward the spine, its cavity filled
With stones — perhaps the body

Would not fear high wind,
The press of other bodies, the way
The sun divests objects of weight.
And the moon. Turns questions
To insect wings. They drink light
And release it, wings like individual
Rain, tiny bodies of wire. How many

Flowers I could have collected
For you. How well I know
What can be supplanted with foil,
What can, from a distance,
Entice. Understand, I am intact.
The tongue is metal, and the heart.
Say what you will about
Absolutes. I have seen
Walls open like petals with enough
Subterranean force.

Being Glass

This is music: Birds scratch a line from treetop
to roof. The struck spine rings
like a sealed room. A person could identify leaves
through the shoulder blades. The tongue
glacial, the arms strips of light.
From the right direction, houses billow and curve.

Years later, the man awoke,
not remembering his eyes. They were a particular color,
he knew, and when he wore a certain shirt,
he could leave the house without shaving.
The woman, too, once had eyes.
He painted them for her, the only detail of her face
rendered mistaken. Snow falls,
and the picture is grainy.
I am old, he thinks, though this doesn't help.

Things That Seldom Remain in Place

Ghosts peel from the wallpaper. They turn to foxes,
run red to the trees. Weather knots
at the corners of sleep and will not recede.
Who can see a stranger's wrist
and not have regrets? The scent of wild orange
invokes memory benign; sliced lime
calls forth pleasing thoughts best forgotten.

Girls by the roadside become foxes most of all:
The warrior sped down a familiar street and entered a field.
Retainers vanished as soon as he spoke.

A spectacle of disbelief: the merchant sells glimpses
of a parrot that the emperor
refused. It swallows hot coals without choking.
Or belief: a woman with broken combs in her hair
upends a man's gaze. She leads him beneath the house.
He sees a palace curtained with rooms.
Two weeks later, he emerges, his back bent
from stooping, a figure recognizable only by voice.
The man had cheated his tenants.
Foxes scratched at the gates of the yard.

The sun, too, is a taken thing. Across an ocean,
a man's sister stops speaking,
leaving this voice to stand for everything lost.
Bathing women draw their robes shut
like blinds. The bowl on the mantel
fills with avowals: seven antique marbles,
a clam shell wrapped with thread.

Having forgotten the difficult words,
mostly I greet and agree. Memories of hands

wrest the air from this room: How can anyone
speak? The fox blends into silence.
A snake wrapped around a bell
takes the echo with her when she leaves.

Geisha Considered as Making

Outside the door, voices range,
Each a petal barred from another life

And brought here. Do you see
The door is torn? I eat in rooms without windows

And refuse to paint my lips. Once
I wore red and served an open hand,

Was young and blew into reeds.
Now all the frames contain wings.

They move in my sleep. Did you imagine
This fine erosion? I entered your body

As night enters all the lit corners of a room
And lasts. Sky presses the trees

Back into the earth. I loved my own
roundness and loss. Do not forget:

There are webs and webs between us,
Tight-woven and clean.

The light is your voice, a backdrop
Of sound outside the door.

My body can hold it, shoulders bare
As the ground that used to harbor

Our steps. Without warmth in this season,
How do you think your fine mouth could exist?

Calculate Where to Begin

The crickets in full regalia tonight,
The light bulb whining a lucid
Kind of absence. I have heard wires vibrate inside.
Certainly have seen moths trapped
And alight, the human heart
Reducing need to a mechanics of sound.

Eucalyptus sharpens its leaves.
At the water, I'm sure, shells press imperfect
Globes into sand, regardless of whether
We detect them or not. As children
We heard feet on the staircase and thought
The house was breathing. The dead
Shook themselves loose from whatever
Had kept them. There will be time
For rephrasing this later. When we trace
Our own suppleness and try to forget.

Gloves filled with water really do
Look like hands. If the light
Were partial, I could offer a heart
In ink. You could say it were mine,
and indeed I would love you,
The parts I remember dislocated, clean.

Topographical Concern

This is the architecture I recall: Roof thatched,
Shoes on the step. The rain today is the same,

Except the air holds it, a damp veil at night,
With the house dark and shut.

Today, clouds become a separate kind of skin,
Blunt, fragrant as the trees. Voices in the field

Divide the air with their cries. Sounds rise
Above the ground, and I ask you not

To forget, though speech now is thick
On the tongue. Umbrellas open giant petals,

Figures below them sketched into stems.
I remember sticks igniting as one. One form blends

To another: Our skin is not definitive enough.
On unnamed streets, each house re-speaks the rest,

The method of recall lost in the smell of night leaves.
Who says the figure by the wall is not plaster,

In the end? Speak very clearly.
I cannot hear your voice through the din.

Anatomy of Resemblance

On beds in different rooms, or distant,
a woman shifts the angle of her foot.
In the light, her hair changes from red
to the dresser's dull wood, a signature
begun the moment her stocking
slipped just enough to remind us she is there.

Can you hear the birds? I can't pronounce
their name in any language. That echo
over the wire is not a door closing:
No one has entered the room.
There is no reason not to trust me,
no memory, even, of the right word now,
but it begins in the manner of *Signal,*
as in *Traffic* or *Truth*.

In the painting, a person of a certain age,
alone, is not grounds for alarm.
I mean, *In this country*. Or, *Whom did you touch
before me?* Most of all, ivy
doesn't litter the shelves as I promised
it would. I promised soft leaves
and give even less, one hand already
reaching toward an exit. That bright sign
in the hall, yes, is a memorable thing.

Postcard—a memory carried in the body

The place between the ribs you thought was silent,
Was yours. How many maps I could show you,

Chronicles of the way the systems work:
Silvered veins, the blind crawl of muscles in sleep.

For the terrains you've seen, I give you mine.
Once I welcomed skirts spread like bright

Water, and any permanent mark. Words break in the air:
Husks of small worlds,

With nothing inside. *Tell me again
What you thought you preferred.* Memory

Eclipses the sun, her swift delineations.
Each winter, light the furnace

And be equally stunned by lit dust,
The musk of pages open on the floor.

This is the myth of repair, the skyline,
Still, a barrier of trees. Tonight the snow

Is not enough to hold us, nor we
Warm enough for it to remember our shapes.

Equation

Reframe the words and this picture
inhales. Witness the microscope,
narrowing on the eye until we see
only particles that swim

in dark light. They are blind.
How to account for ice in small piles,
sudden by the door, and rain
uncontainable eight thousand miles away?

Sometimes two lives coincide,
in water frozen and water
withholding the ground from our steps.
The fruit inside is bitter, skin sweet,

and both are eaten at once.
The teacup painted in pomegranate
and leaves—one touch to the lips
mars it, the body exhales

onto any surface
it can. Insects whittle their limbs
to hairs, all for music,
for habit. The heart in the mouth
another terrible seed.

Recalling the Start

Pottery arrives in pieces like sleep. Ninety-five nights
Of listening: The clock strikes against air.

We measure *forward* in minutes
Captured in speech. The grass is unbearably wet.

On the phone, one word then another skids
Beneath the tongue. There is comfort in this emptiness.

And please will you touch me. Mynah birds
Draw sounds from the air, but not yet.

Now, there is nothing but fruit, dark seeds staring
From feathers like oil. Will you remember

This tone, when the actual language is lost? The simple
Logic of a compass in the rain:

Where one is, another is not, despite talk
Of the stars (nearly the same in two places).

Trees smelled sharper before: The radio played
Next door, one sentence, no hesitation

For breath. Once more: One figure on the balcony,
The smaller below — from a distance,

Barely bigger than shells. Do you see?
They are not homes, only something from which

A softness has been taken. Did you touch my hair,
Or was that hand mine? Intentions shift

Under water in leaves. Three words
For various kinds of dividing, bottles on the windowsill

Fervently blue. Once a year, bells ring if there is someone
To sound them. If the snow melts,

Something unforeseen will be given.
If the snow melts, something unforeseen will be given.

Before the River Freezes in Place

1.
The sky is water, and yes, I am thirsty.
The camera catches an angle
I do not recall. To remember more
than a cupful at a time is a sad kind
of longing: First the bird caught the fish.
The fish struggled and all came
to a halt. This is good.
He traced my mouth with his hand.

2.
One day a flower opened: Petals unraveled
to twine on the floor. Children woke
speaking garbled, in tongues. That day,
I discovered the difference
between water from a cup and from
careful hands: only one way
works. Before the river stopped running,
we melted wax into tapers,
gathered tin for when we'd have none.

3.
Five children perched on the fence.
At the first crack of thunder,
everyone flew. Air before rain
is blanketed and thick, warm as a child's bed.
And if the figure is small,
the room will seem empty and safe.
I am not small, and the river
didn't halt. Men still dry leaves for tea.

4.
See the girls dance around the flagpole
in dresses. Arms curved like rope,

they dance on salt. The earth
is clean, the stars cut
through the skin, then work their way
into the blood. When it all
hits your heart, will you explode? I have.

5.
Sing me the story where lightning
divides the tanager in two.
Each half beak opens, and wind pulls night
from inside the two mouths.
Are you looking for comfort? No matter
how you ask it, those two sides of sky
do not become one. There are people
wanting to be covered by night.
There is a bird-shaped space
the color of light.

Yield to This

My daughter dreams of persimmons. What a wife she will make,
this shadow who invents no new arrangements
of dishes. She cannot serve tea. Flowers decline
in the vase her visitor offers. He has traveled some distance
simply to hear her speak. At eighteen, her beauty

unmarred as the fruit she dreamed of, so pliable I could not see her
and not think of death. After that, a girl learns to arrange
her rooms like a song. The mats without dust,
as if no foot has bruised them. I hear
she walks outside without shoes. No one will have her.

When I visited last, her doorway smelled of citrus dried
in a bowl. In ten years, she will nail blankets
over her windows to frighten the cold. No body will warm her.
Twice, she laughed when she was young,

in a voice like a marsh bird's, metal against the spine.
Who will unwrap her when no one discerns
whether anything lies underneath? Unclothed,
she could be breath alone, and breath keeps nobody
warm. Will you touch her hair for me,

will you remind her I am here? She is rare
as the tree that appears most dead in the spring.
Her eyes seeds. Will you cover her walls
with silk? Beauty seen produces more
of the same. This is what it is like to be a mother

of ghosts. I fear my hand could press
right through her skin. If she sleeps, lower a cage
about her head. If she does not sleep, how will I see her?
Did you receive the fruit I sent in dry, gold grass? Oil like the sun.
Respectfully, awaiting response.

II

The Field of Choice. And Choosing.

All that remains is a lamp with green
at its steepled crown,

a room in which she did not belong
and knew it.

Here, then, is the shame.
The orange[1] did not belong on the plate,
hunger *in absentia*.

At that time, the clock spoke its *remain here,*
too heavy for the air around it
to hold. First, take a breath:

At age X, still I cannot swim,[2]
the world having no shape without eyes,
nothing easily defined.

On film, that blur is either a bare shoulder
or part of a lamp.

The pure window / from the inside / from the inside / throw it open.[3]

I do not want to be photographed like that:
The first roll I destroyed.

---

1. Blood, always blood
   The color blue like blue
   Accustomed to thirst, the orange's incessant explosion

   At three years of age, the infant saw an orange arranged on a blue and white dish. At that moment, he knew both the sun and his own shining mortality.

2. *She does not need them,* the mother said, generally meaning the eyes, ears, & most of touch and taste.

3. A. Kawata

Before 1195, the *field of choice*
was lacquer[4]: ornamental boxes, small stones.

Treasure had nothing to do
with the face, eyebrows redrawn—the curve of a fan,
teeth filled in with black.[5]

Physiognomists decided: *An important boy,*
meant for ruled things.[6]
Or did they mean, *Shining but not necessarily real?*

Imprints on the lawn
could have been anyone, Love,

Or no such crime of entry
and depart.[7]

---

4. The slight rounding of the lid gives this flat box a graceful shape that is en-
   hanced by the dense scrollwork in "polished lacquer" in which *kalavinka*
   spirits hover among plant scrolls.

5. Because (the boy's) teeth were slightly decayed, his mouth was charmingly
   dark when he smiled. One almost wished that he had been born a girl.

   —*The Tale of Genji*

6. Somehow news of the sage's remarks leaked out, though the emperor him-
   self was careful to say nothing.

7. One day, a woman went to sleep at noon and awoke to find a man in her
   room. Usually quiet, she leapt out of bed and yelled at him, "Get out of
   my house!" He paused by the dresser, bowed, and left the apartment. The
   woman had not looked directly at his face. When questioned later, she said,
   "In case I knew him, I didn't want that shame between us when we met."
   He had come in through the kitchen window, she said. He followed the
   same path out.

In a second picture, yellow skies
prefigure gilding. Indeed,

1000 years later, ornaments
still retain their gold. Copper inlay
on the shoulders suggests, of course,

Carnations. Birds
freeze in the sky. We pluck them,

small berries, not knowing
otherwise
how to remember the scene.

Being Glass, the Glint of Sun

Birds around the shops pick at glass
As if it were food. How beautiful is the scattered,
How impossible to recall. A monk
Whose name I've forgotten carved a tunnel
Between cities, penance for sins
Closely recalled. Small horses
Walked through that mountain,
One side a mouth facing the sea. The grass

That grew was long and tuned
If touched to the lips. This is music: A small hammer

Hits stone. Sparks are untenable,
But see how the breastplate
Alights. When light strikes, the burnished arm
Warms. Birds clutter the base, small storms
Of two and three. The heart makes
Such a noise that no one can sleep. Is there
Nothing to do but repeat *I remember,* to wait
For quiet to lower its jar.

The Border Between

There is oil on the mouth, candle burnt past-wick,
the temperature gauge on the wall

reading zero: There is no way to measure
this roundness, this reaching forward

of the best unsaid. Lamplight on skin.
There is something more spacious

in enclosure, which asks no choice but one,
but done with passion. Each fiber knowing

the need to fill. One uncracked cup: Know to lift
and when. There is oil on the hem

and the clothes torn to leaves. A bird's wing
shorn and left on the lawn, its twin

half a length away. The body a kind of corsage
on grass past green, last guess of rain.

Reading zero: Your eyes all one color
in faded light. Unbelievable.

Round. The improbable collects
where we least expect it,

sound pressed into folds of skin.
Asking a question is most like a swallowing-back,

the answer trapped in bone, instinctive,
half-known in wanting-sounds

dredged from sleep: We are least aware
and least wary, wanting to touch the lintel and when.

Gift

The birds that chattered in the trees above the school
have left us with the sound of wings and the smell of smoke
in our hair. For three nights now, only one star
has graced the curve of the moon. The sky is silenced:
We cannot move, who gauge our way by stories
lit above our heads. Before dawn, a uniformed man
tossed a wire loop around a stray dog's neck.
For the first time, I remembered my fear. This is a city
where teams of men shout at once, then return the fields
to their usual calm. No letters arrive. The doll left as a gift
for the previous tenant is faceless as I am, as pale.
Robed in mustard and red, she has no features,
her head smooth as a spool. I love her best
for she has no arms: She holds another no better than I.
The doll will crumble if left at the door. Already,
ash powders her hair. At night, we call our solitudes
equal, one as still as milk, the other gentle
as the dust that mutes her. We have become a town
spoken of in stories. One forgets
there are actual stones to bruise the knees when we fall.

Prime Movement and Other Divinations

1.
The flower moved first. I tell you, I watched it,
waiting for the moment when belief
would consist of an egg-shaped stone in the hand.

You can predict tomorrow by the direction
of roots, cilia at first, then long slender
mouths. *What is it you wanted*

to know? The sky shifted its skirts. I did not move.
Even the tin cup on the windowsill stilled.

2.
Bare wood is best, unevenly cut. A candle
just above the drawer holding silk, and even the corners
are ridged.

When the woman's limbs turned to wood,
did you ask her how
she managed touch? Did you ask her about *small gnat*

and *fire?* Cut any tree open, and know its age
precisely. Divide the silk into appropriate
and not. How simple to recall

when leaves barely bend, when the room echoes
its own kind of sleep.

3.
No room for anger when the floor gathers
what it can. The story begins in a cage:

by the front porch, nothing grows
except skeletal weeds. Dust soaks the color from wood.

In three strokes, even the bed can be rewritten.
Tell me. Does water gather underground,
or do plants pull it to the surface

in threads? A divining stick would tell you:
I, too, am a watery thing.

4.
Cracks in the wall point north, the direction
the pillow must face.
Is this not order,

despite roots dividing the soil
in ways? One stem of ivy does not sleep.
I know

three methods to open a mollusk,
fifteen uses for salt.
The body is only as clean
as it remembers to be, meaning *this one,*

meaning *small fire.* Its surface is a feast
of small moving things: *Microscopia,*
I am for you, jeweled.

What Magnitudes Sing Us

There is this between them, quiet assent.
An alleyway folded, gravel upon dirt:
Who alone can follow it,
a ribbon nailed, a curve on the door.
Once the grass sang to a god of its making,
then withered into the crack
from which it had sprung, green and frightening
as the message between them,
curved in the wake of their footsteps,
the one clear breath
of cloth against skin. And it isn't summer,

but it could be, there. Can you hear the words
between them, slicing foliage
off trees, but gently,
accosting the air for what it has not given,
what it cannot commend. Every word
is effort but sweet—
mangoes and salt could not make them
more content than they are,

or less. This moment, as the dirt
upswallows the grass, and the stones
enclose heat and become
their own bodies—they tell themselves—
safer for it. If they have not wondered

which shadows hang carefully
on the trees, and which among them
their own figures have hung,
they will not ask each other now,
as the day claims more than is merciful,
as fruit dries in strips under glass.

Affair Ending in Touch

Light fell from the hand the very statue
Dimmed beside it

They open the birds because they have to, people are waiting

To eat, and drink
Cannot fill the glass the way always   (I imagined it would)

First there was song, then the horse's eye swam up like that
(Bluer than they said water was)

Bluer than they said
And *Is she the right size for this?*

And am I? Silk only is jade and nobody asks
From what city it came   (Please)

I have watched every move and always the clock
Scraping against—

(Tired of greetings, the woman went to bed)

Love, the book says, is pivot and wait.

Curtains open and alone on the screen
A white etching reels, one arm extended toward something

              (Unclear)

Did you ever consider *How often*
Anyone wanted—

In the final instance,
No shadow, no proof that the figure existed even

Only   (*To touch*)

Because the Cup Is Furred, I Cannot Drink

I split the apple in half and ate each half in turn,
Then the seeds. Gathered as many people as I could,
Then slipped between buildings,
Away. Women gather their skirts above the knees
To cross water, right? I walked straight through,
Forgetting I couldn't swim. I couldn't swim,
But once a friend tried to teach me,
Holding my body afloat. Because I put fear in the dish
With the keys and any stray coins.
Because fear, anyway, ripples at the edges of things.
Even the ochre-colored cloth got wet.
The day darkens in heat. I gathered the stones,
Their lapidary speech. In the garden, stone
Paths curved like streams around flowers,
Gently bent. I walked where I could, needing shade.
I do have a will. It rises like speech in the night
When insects are still and the fan cuts an arc
Through thick air. It collects in the palms of the hands
When I sit very still. Because the plates were expensive,
I ate off the ground. Because the lock didn't work,
I buried the key. I gathered you up, mottled in my hands,
And held us to the light. I gathered the sun
By mistake and set it down swiftly. At that time,
I spoke in tongues. Because the woman
Could not scream, she wondered how to be safe.
Because the cup is furred, I cannot drink.
Cats collect beneath the azalea. One plant withered,
The rest holding on. Soil beneath ivy the color of tea:
Even the spoon is not immune to this softness.

Museum Rehearsal

1.
If the pear tree did explode as they say, what happened to the
       hospital,
bittered rooms. And the people,

Wearing orange and orange again
                                        —Or was that fire?

What ranged inside the empty rooms, what raged outside them:
Only weather, licking paint off walls,
muting the staircase,

                                   All the usual

Clamor. So why did ghostly forms collect in the corners at night and

Have you heard the figures speak?

And why?
Which language did *the one by the bed*
                                        Use?

This is a normal hand, requisite and clean.
If you can see through it, if fingers are not distinct,
then clearly

2.
After Kawabata

Moths halo the light, but the woman doesn't notice,
combing black horsehair and weaving it
into her own. *See? I'm a new person now.*
He can't look. In this season, everything around him
falls. Just this morning, he swept seven moths

onto the grass, wings green and paper-thin.
Insects die on the table, and worse, stick to the powder
she spreads on her neck. *She is a geisha,* he thinks,
and pictures her warm and drunk in his bed.
At parties, her sleeves fill with cigarettes
the ambassadors give as gifts. She divides
the tobacco between them. But the insects.
They die at the first tremor of cold.
They die against a backdrop of trees and night.
He thinks of his wife and her collection
of seeds. He remembers her nightgown,
the thick coverlet on the bed. *This shade
or this?* the woman asks, holding identical reds.
He points without thinking. *I'm yours,*
she says and hollows her arms to receive him.

3.
In Japan, a man imagines snow.   Remember

The bulbs, sent from another country, doomed to break

black tulips, bred into submission. How a flower can furl

                                        A circle that small.

                            Cut open slightly

With a knife, would sound escape? Would life,

In all its jars? All the waking dreams of breath in another country,

A white bed stiff with sheets. What exactly holds

                                        The patients in place?

In the letter of the law,

          There must be something about beds.

4.

Documentary

Here is the room as you left it. Clothes in the attic multiply and speak, their tongues like roots pushed quickly, but deep. Do not think of me like this, blankets undone, the floor cold and spare. Wearing blue to reflect what is holy. *In this way,* someone said, *you will be protected.* Improbable skin. Letters come like small animals, curled in relative warmth. Their alphabets shift when I turn.

Kakera you call the stories I tell. Bits of nothing at all. In this year, and following, and after. When the clothes are gone, what of the body remains? A woman I knew thought that her father cut her children to dolls. Lay with her and scattered—what came. Why is she here, and in which collection would you place her?

Birds mimic each other's cries. When I walked in the snow, stars scattered like teeth. All else disappeared. The words you taught filled the candle's small bowl until no one could read them. In this case, is the candle a silencing? Except—how the light plays on your face. What sings now, where you are?

On the first day, the world split like a pear, seeds intact. Don't worry. Language rises to the surface of matter. This is why I remember your touch. When the building caught fire, statues filed out. The sky opened and closed, or was that the trees? By the end, all drama was light. In your absence, I promise—our faces did not dance.

Notes

1: To the past

This is the season when skin sloughs off, when snakes return
to shapes they left behind
last spring. *What can fit?* The accident of desire
drifts across the water, wordless at such

distance. Last night, fifty crows circled the pines,
a cacophony of wings. Last night, the pear tree went up in flames.
Pears burst in the heat, each a world
blind to the rest. Birds answer each other's cries.

Birds collect around the berries, crests brilliant
as tongues. Desire hums in the current, in the way the river ripples
two ways at once. Bark peels, sticks form an illusion
of ground. Even red berries

withdraw in cold. In this season, gray sky
blends to gray water. *What was it we were due to be gathering?*
The word for shelter just inches past reach.

2: Of language

Kakera (see *kake*): 1. a fragment; a (broken) piece; a chip. 2. a crack; a
fissure; a flaw.

The character for *kake* (a selection) means: a lack, a gap; to neglect,
fail in, omit; broken piece (of glass, etc.); yawn; want, dearth, famine;
absence, default; hairline; ullage; unqualified person; missing num-
ber; damage; collapse.

Shelter (synonyms): *cover, retreat, refuge, asylum, sanctuary, haven. Sanctuary* denotes a sacred or inviolable place. *Haven* can apply to an anchorage or broadly to any sheltered area.

Geisha: a flaw; a (covered) piece; a fissure; asylum in different (combinations); famine; a sacred piece (of glass, etc.); dearth; the condition of absence; can apply to an anchorage or more broadly; to omit; the amount of liquid in a container (missing number, want) lost during shipment; a fissure; *akubi;* unqualified to protect.

Postcard—Without Grace

Mosquitoes unstrung the night. Twice sleep broke,
you said, *Enough.* Then the night—

And the many of waiting three hours for headlights
and swift, thorough sleep. Who knows

what can be understood later from this, my hair grayed
at the nape, nails growing like roots in the dark.

The apartment above opened and closed
all night: The hinge spoke. Once I told you

everything I knew in a language
you did not speak. This is love, is division,

a pile of memories catalogued like stars.
What seems to burn a trick of time,

of loss. From this angle I remember you best
and which photo most resembles—

Trees smell differently this many miles away.
When you call there are sirens, machinery

neither can name. From here on, history is nothing
but waiting. The background

panoramic, larger than life. From this far away,
which speck are you. I am this one, I'm sure. I am here.

III

Gold Filigree Sharp on the Neck

1.
Fifteen origami cranes, gold filigree sharp on the neck.
If the pattern were repeated,
hibiscus on the skin of a person remembered. Over and over,
I thought—on the balcony,
a walnut-colored form and again *a form*—
How to distinguish one object from the next?

2.
The Mona Lisa stolen and returned in 1913. We have to decide
what is *functional,* what not. Begin:
The group met in a balconied house,
spoken in clover and spring. Once again,
the atom split and deciphered,
clear as water, as the first words of love
on the lips of a girl
just young enough to say it.

3.
The pagoda is deserted. We photograph
all that exists of it. See, the bottle of rum really was
speckled like that, red and black,
an entire spread of cards. How green the moon
on which so much of secrecy
rests. Instead, the stars soldered in place,
houses lulled to submission:

4.
The sum of it all another *Vive la*—painted on eggshell,
a crowd gathered to see.
The best part of accidents is the story constructed,
snow gleaming blue, light from a garage
printing its *yes* on the asphalt below.
Who ever thought
a person could speak like that?

5.
The woman did. Her eyes shone, could not be
reproduced. On this day, *a certain blue*
was invented. On this night,
the mirror explodes
into cranes. A pewter flask on the shelf,
the sharp curve of an arm.
This alone could make a dinner
right. Lilies traced in olive, and sprawling.
The postcard lost in the cloud mass, unharmed.

Conversation in Likeness

The moon drops a decibel, insects
speak in its place. I am yours,

irresolute. If *mercury*
and *blue* are the same word,

differently spelled, I understand
only this: the touch and sever of chase,

the automatic retrieval of whatever falls
first. *Do not forget,* you say,

and I hold the yes in the making,
a pebble that grows if tended,

for damage or display.
Will you live between them,

curled and waiting? If so, know
that my hand will go with you, and an eye.

The rest stands apart.
One word and the next drops into the place

where memory is a circular field,
a soft white mass like sleep.

Soon only crickets between us
in common. We speak in their repetition:

Each night, one match struck and again
until light is too great to see them.

Until snow falls and extinguishes tiny legs.

Hôtel des Pyrénées

after an essay by Charles Simic

As the story goes, men dunk bread in Arabian wine,
fill the gold scales with messages home.

Tell Daria this—
How cool the leaves.

Upstairs, a bedroom resonant with chairs, stockings discreet
in a bundle near the door.

It begins with a shop twisting the hour to baskets,
a reverie of crates. We have sold snap beans

to Napoleon,
blanketed the palace with a quick blur of silk.

*

How often I have courted small leaves.

In the window box,
cinders where nothing will grow.

A dream of mint lights the north side of the room:

The bed, suddenly, reticent as tin.

*

On the balcony, rain insists
a world partway beyond our making.

Each maple leaf a school of urgency:
Poysonous mineralls held to wide mouth o'rstride.

Red hands at dusk become a dim fire.
No letters have arrived.

*

Tell Daria this—

Some knowledge *must* have led the carriage
here. Voices condense into cufflinks,

a gem at the throat.
Did this room once belong to a *woman of the court?*

The moment becomes
nearly graspable,
                                    an object

held to light. Resist
the fluted glasses, the linger of cloves.

                            Guests descend the gold staircase

like shadows—

proof of solidity elsewhere,
but near.

Oblivion Fruit

They say that animals forget their homes
if not called three times
before dawn. I believe because speech

comforts better than this drying marsh.
Answers spring forth like strange orange flowers
in glass. In a field behind the gate,

grass grows waist-high, all dead,
stalks with a dark umber spread, wide as both
of my hands. Even the weeds anticipate cold.

They say there's a fruit to forget
the arms of a love, to erase even the face.
What then? Nothing changes: The pain is just

another green that fades according to season.
Across the river, two women fight in silence
over ginkgo nuts. They touch

the single tree between them, invoking
whatever governs the fruit: Fall quickly,
fall quietly, in a place each can easily find.

A History of Vinegar and Reprieve

1.
This is *the basis of electronics,* light contracting to ice outside the
        window,
Glass pears catching all of it, giving

Little away. This is the novel where two people argue what *antipodes*
        means,
A collection of sources:

And the man said, O Lord.

Everyone repeated. "When three people speak at once,
Ice has grown too deep

To bear."

All current, all catching light.

*

The Story of A

Came to America in 1955. Spoke in colors attainable and clear. Lived
in a room on the second floor, a full suite, barely recalled. Occasion-
ally drank, but does not say what. Often drank coffee and talked about
numbers. Entertained women? Unknown. Piloted a small airplane,
married late. Lived in numbers and chairs. Remembers having *only a
language in common;* geography apart. Begat five children who begat
none at all. Belief in mysterious causes: Reluctant. There is a way to
do things that *does not cause harm.* Rose bushes planted, world nearly
in shape.

2.
The bread is hard, the small room harboring
Particular warmth. The story begins on a boat with a young man,

A woman in a ginger-colored hat.
Whether the figure was bronze or *cast from human form*

Or simply a person, shading her eyes from water on light: Debate
Postponed. Pomegranates carved in the general shape

Of keys, white wine in a dark red dish. Begin again
Completely, the cabaret opening its doors

Always the first time. Memory leaving no ash on the table.
Together we entered and are entering still,

I in a dark red skirt, you either statue
Or speech. Animals line up on copper fields:

Chile breathes three times and the smallest insects flee. This is
    account,
A walnut cracked carefully on its seam, philology

Perfect inside.
But there really were fields, and copper rose to the surface —

The whole village shone in orange and sleep.

*

The Story of B

Walked into a lake to let a hat float on the surface. To touch a land-
scape leaves nothing permanent behind, they say. *But the shadow of
the hat on the water* — And he just a child at the time. A forest grew
around the shadow, and men hung like strange leaves from the trees.
This is later — No matter when all that is left are the toads crawling
toward land and a sister quiet with a gun. *But is a party the place to*

perform such a feat? They say she went outside. By this time, he said nothing at all. *Angel,* he called her. *The same* he called himself. White powder skirted the trees and left a shadow on the lake.

3.
The table is bare now. Let the film begin:

This is the landscape, deposited in ore.
This is the sound of anything buried.

Memory levies no sheen on the table.
This is the difference between vinegar and mint.

Across the water, the first notes of *Der Nibelung* strike.
Seven trees harvest their leaves all at once.

This is twine to wind around the flask.
This is the pomegranate: Wood.
This is the figure: Speaks.

Seven pears in a white canvas slip:
An introduction of *illness* and *reprieve*.

*

The Story of C

Named for a famous murderer and raised near a river. Fears alligators and death of natural causes. Dreams: vivid. Hasn't been home in six years. In Panama, one day each year children dress as adults. They paint body hair on and stare at the camera or smile. Ties a cross on her wrist. Favorite color: Red. Favorite drink: Anything clear. Fell in love with a married Slovakian. In summer, eats only shaved ice. *A*

strange pain between the head and neck. Distrusts flowers and devices.
Gives away bracelets. Will not regret.

4.
In the rendering, the figures speak as one,
Seven languages, seven ways of breaching *please*

And *go away*. There must be a way to contain things
So they don't break apart:

Voice clocked at 1100 feet per second.
The village in vinegar, asleep.

Persimmons and a Kind of Regret

The flowers are copper, tin to the touch,
but you must not touch them. The orange
thorns didn't change much in the telling,
but the lace was all imagination,
texture added to indigo and white.

People here speak in strung vines
and twig, our last conversation inscribed
on a leaf too sharp to ignore. Which man
painted that leaf, and could a strong wind
decrease it? Voice is more easily erased:

already, ours fade into the stem. In time,
even touch grows bare and thin.
The background speaks, always speaking:
Where were you born? — *Blue.*
But two people talk as one. Which answer

do you trust? And if these persimmons
unpinned from their stems,
would this moment, too, follow
in course? Gentle-edged speech uproots
more than it holds. I have tried.
Rain washes some I hope
but not all of it away.

Survival & Disembodied Existence

Fifteen black flowers narrow in the vase,
no water
to speak of. An electrical storm:

Sparks jump from the coil on the stove,
tiny flame. Made things
are safest untouched. Try

saying *Come back,* and watch
people reel without turning,
coats petaled in wind.

Unbodied, the ghost crosses space
so much like itself
its shape becomes fish, slicing water,

feeling it flame in back
and then heal.
Shifting air with air until only the wind

notes its passing. What is untouched
unfurls, surprising as breath.
There is, there must be, warmth from this becoming.

Mistranslate (Because Meaning Is Not Enough)

1.
In the lull and hum of your voice
saying come

home as if your body were house
and arbor and mine

the vine that drinks dark air. Pink flowers
somebody's version of skin.

Would that your pretty pictures
were mine and believe

that when I think of you I see a solid thing.

2.
Cut open you'd be
rings infinitely small until the center,

a mar. Most of all I have heard
your wait and translated it

as I pleased, saying, *My fault*
and *Of course.*

I like simplicity, its single weight.
I like the word *fault* for its power

to fit within the hand and consume.
Here is my arm and shoulder,

my throat and every word.

3.
When I spoke of the martyrs,
I cherished most the eyes
looking up. They comb the sky
like a child glancing at the ceiling

for an answer he cannot know.

4.
He does not know it, being small,
but the body will betray him.

Its illness and desires,
even the hunger that means

nothing to him now. The left hand
has never known the right:

They speak a different tongue.

5.
In the current equations,
the fingers are not enough.

What reaches us is not necessarily
anger or love. Interpret at will.

Swallow your eyes, your tongue,
and leave the scaffolding

behind. This is your final instance
of choice. You barely hear

who gathers the familiar to call.

To Recant What Is Needed

I am back to things, having found
that I need them to fall and to break
to remind that I too can collect

and be collected, another set of rules,
a conceivable form. I said
we were nothing without speech.

Today I don't care for radio static
or the flutist's beautiful name. Know
that I'll learn to love the door

as I love the rest of the world,
with reservation. I claimed
to mistrust form, now welcome a space

defined at least partly by scent. This much
I understand: the broken clock,
its hands held together

by the coat on the floor. A favorite word
begins with the mouth and ends
with the hands loosely clasped. Begins with a question

and wanders to a stop, having forgotten
its riddle for the coat or the leaf
that calls the mind back.

Five Stories of Demand

Last night there was a scream last night,
but whether man, woman, or beast, I could not
say. Night tore into blades of grass,
and only a voice can do that
rightly. Last night, later, five words
for help of some kind: *kyuujo, ooen, sukuu,*
and on. Four corners and the tip of the roof
and who says a building cannot be connected
like that, all lines straight, the weight sinking
into earth. There are many ways to bury
what is wanted. One sister chose the mind
and carried a shovel for proof. The grandmother
sang on the radio and now sings yes the earth
will match and flare. The voice
has stopped, but the night remains in pieces.

Once upon a time lived a woman who split herself in two, one to live
with a man she was forbidden, the other to work in her father's home.
Both were happy, we presume, and shone under certain wings. The
two met years later (watched by the man, concealed in a bush with
their child) and melded into one. Her name begins like this: *Sei——*.
For hundreds of years, we ask, Which figure was real? The answer
measures our pacing. And yet to ask: Did they touch hands before
both disappeared? The answer measures our——. A leaf rises improb-
ably from the center of a lake.

Two small cats on the windowsill, still disjointed
As the story goes, not far from the temple lived a fox alone
Batting one then the other and the small heads turn
And needing mischief, stole a fisherman's eel and ran with it
But neither looks down. One could be the other save for a ribbon
Twined around its neck. Unable to shake the eel off or see

They know nothing of gravity. The window is high
Gon (he was called) tore to his burrow and only then
Hedged by brick below. They shift, a many-legged beast
Could break its neck and eat. In the next story
Fierce, without a name. This begins nine kinds of falling.

1. A farmer's wife blackens her teeth with pitch
2. All day and night she begged for eels to eat and he
3. Climb to the roof, the festival unfolds!
4. Drums collect and chrysanthemums drown underfoot
5. Has stolen them. What regret, he thinks, what
6. The temple bell is ringing. Has Hyojuu's wife disappeared?
7. When figures straggle past in white, he sees his mistake
8. If she died asking for eels and only on his account
9. Farther on, the blacksmith's wife combs her hair

Beneath an umbrella of root, the day turns on its axis.
Clouds gather as they will and retreat
among the trees. In the telling, all moments
press toward the lucid, each a single stone,
without fear. To listen and not are instances
of waiting. If the eyes fill like branches
lit with crows, who will receive them?
The farthest buildings vanish completely
in mist. In this season of quiet disappearance,
rain only comforts, its voice like tin birds,
and many, and more. One pear without a bowl
to contain it: Unpolished globe, bright juice.

First Received

This wind is sweet with nothing I can name.
Crushed leaves smell thick and dark as letters
between us, bitter to taste. This is a month
of watching fields court the comparative warmth
of the ground. I hear your voice in strange places,
as bats swim around branches, and water
draws night toward its sheen.

The statue in the garden shapes an indifferent gaze.
The leaves around her breathe citrus
and dusk. I think of you when the last light
glints off the roof tiles. I see their order
as one you would admire; from this distance,
delicate and strong as veins in grass.

The pond offers nothing it hasn't received,
reflecting the gate and this path. A god, it swings
between Tantalus and grief, its surface a skin so soft
a hand could break it. Nothing but algae beneath,
an occasional twig. If the leaves
didn't flare and darken on cue, I would think
you've forgotten. Moss collects on the usual side
of trees. In daytime, girls swing, bright birds,
and scrape their shoes on the ground.
They do not fear falling through it, being light
and having no thought of wings.

The Perceptible World

All the dishes are blue, and lovely as eyes,

Eggs shiny and orange in a dish.
Your hands could be wood and are lovelier for this.
Tonight, fill the spaces with anything at all,
Dark strips of seaweed, rice

White as air in the story

Where everything separates in pairs, narrow as twigs.
Decorations dusted with flour or salt:
This distance pulls at the breath.

Without touching, how can I know the guests exist?
My own body solemn in its chair,

Straight as that candle, its own guttered sun.
No flowers on the table,
The center empty as the curve of an arm.

Fish opened to ribs, petaled gray flesh.
The question has vanished, but I remember your eyes,
All pupil at a distance, walnut up close.

I forget all spelling in the roundness of bowls
And how to pry such memories apart.

Malinda Markham was born in California. She received an M.F.A. in Poetry from the University of Iowa and a Ph.D. in Literature and Creative Writing from the University of Denver. Her poetry has been nominated for several Pushcart Prizes and has been published in the *Paris Review, Conjunctions, American Letters & Commentary, VOLT,* the *Colorado Review,* and elsewhere. In 1996, she was awarded a fellowship from the Japanese Ministry of Education and spent the academic year at Saga University. She recently received a grant from the Blakemore Foundation to translate poetry by contemporary Japanese women into English. She teaches in the Foreign Languages Department at Daito Bunka University in Tokyo.